THINGS TO DO WHILE YOU

POO

ON THE LOO

Why farts stink

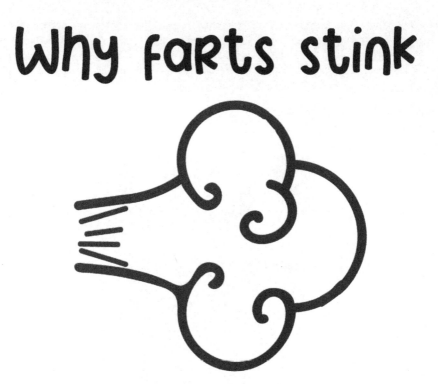

A typical fart is composed of about 59 percent nitrogen, 21 percent hydrogen, 9 percent carbon dioxide, 7 percent methane and 4 percent oxygen. Only about one percent of a fart contains hydrogen sulfide gas and mercaptans, which contain sulfur, and the sulfur is what makes farts stink.

What part of a trilogy is always a stinker?
The turd part.

```
C H A J E E D G O Y B F O B
P L X P S F L O A T E R S O
A E Z A O K G D Y D P I N O
B R E Y U O E L Z O I S W L
G T O W G I P P Y O D J E Y
R E W S A M H I W D U C T I
O T Q E G U Y S E O S P S V
S I R K E E M S X O F S E T
S G U P A W Y T C A U T A V
D Y R S Q E E W R S K U T A
Q U I N T S F E A R I N L N
U C N O Y I J G P B A K E Y
R K E H E V N S H I T N P A
I Y O U S S O K C M S J T H
```

PEE	POOP	STINK
PISS	SHIT	STUNK
URINE	CRAP	GROSS
WEEWEE	DOODOO	YUCKY
WETSEAT	FLOATERS	GAG

*If you complete this search in one visit consult physician.

Bathroom

bath·room   /ˈbaTHro͞om/   noun

A temporary sanctuary for
overwhelmed parents seeking
refuge from their offspring.

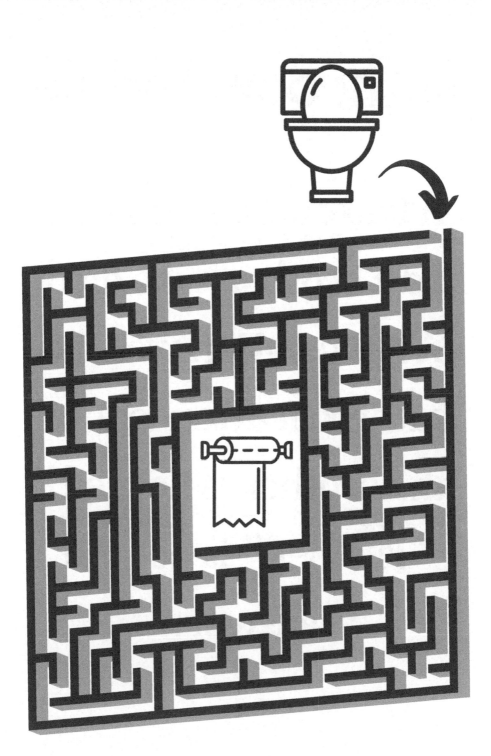

Bathroom Riddle

A bathroom attendant had a brother who died. What relation was the bathroom attendant to the brother who died? "Brother" is not the answer.

The bathroom attendant was the sister of her brother, who died.

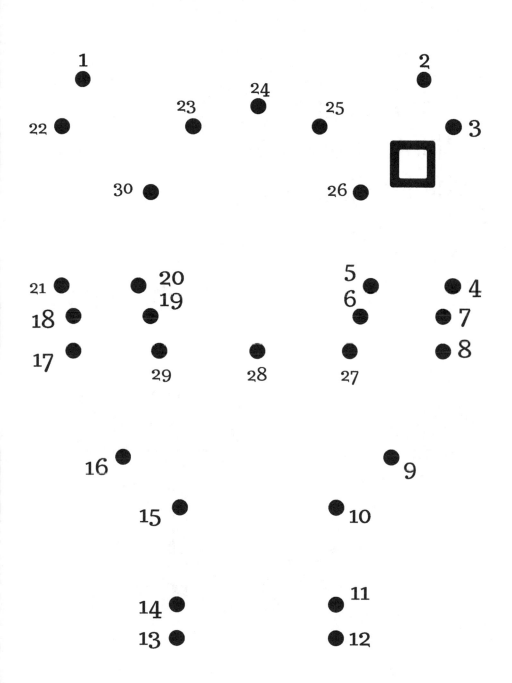

Join the dots at your own convenience

	2						7	3
6	9		3			8		
		1		7	8		6	
7					2	1		5
2			6		1	3		
			7	4				
	1				7			
8		6		1			9	
	7	4		5		2		8

DID YOU KNOW THAT DIARRHEA IS HEREDITARY? IT RUNS IN YOUR GENES.

Farty Facts

Whilst most societies feel that farts should be suppressed in polite company, there are some cultures that celebrate the fart and enjoy it.

If you belong to the Yanomami tribe, you may fart as a greeting.

In China you can get a job as a professional fart-smeller!

Solve these clues.
All answers contain poo

1) Use it to stir your coffee before your morning dump ....

2) A pet animal that goes in the street...................

3) You'd use this to carry a baby ....

4) Water to enjoy when it's hot ....

5) Ghosts and Ghouls...

6) Crossbreed dog...

7) Swirl of water in a river ....

8) Person with very little money ....

9) Use to wash your hair ....

10) Practical joke/not real ....

Don't be Ashamed
to fart while peeing
REMEMBER

Rain sometimes
comes with thunder

★ ★

Recently, I went into a public toilet for a poop.
After sitting down, I heard a voice from the next
cubicle say..

"Hi, how are you?"

I was a little embarrassed but I replied

"I'm fine thanks."

Then the voice asked

"So what are you up to?"

I replied

"Just sitting here, doing the same as you"

Then the voice asked

"Can I come over?"

Annoyed, I said

"Actually, I'm a little busy right now."

The voice then said

"Listen, I'll have to call you back. There's an idiot next door who keeps answering all my questions."

★ ★

Ready. Aim.

Fire

```
S A B P R I W Z P F O D I K
I Y T Z D W A S R I L Z Y S
N E O O E B S J H T H O X L
J S W N O P H Q T O O T S T
K H E G D T S U J I W H A S
O A L U O E H W E L R E D U
S V E J R G A P W E G M R R
R E S O A P M O A T E L M B
N S M C N A P S H S D A X R
Q U E M T K O W U T T K A U
L R A Z O R O Z M I V E H S
V T D B Y M N O L N A B I H
P F L U S H S I N K Y L F O
L E G J A D C O M B H G F Q
```

BRUSH	TOOTHPASTE	SINK	SHOWER
FLOSS	DEODORANT	TOILET	SHAVE
FLUSH	WASH	SHAMPOO	RAZOR
SOAP	TOWEL	COMB	STINK

Finish the Doodle

TYPES OF POOP
(TICK ALL YOUR EXPERIENCES)

- [ ] **CLINGY POOP THAT TAKES 1000 WIPES**
- [ ] **GHOST POOP – YOU FEEL IT BUT CAN'T SEE IT**
- [ ] **GASSY POOP – LOUDER THAN EXPECTED**
- [ ] **THE LOG – NEEDS BREAKING UP WITH AN AXE IN ORDER TO FLUSH**
- [ ] **POWER DUMP – SO FAST YOUR CHEEKS GET SPLASHED**
- [ ] **I WISH I COULD POOP – NOTHINGS HAPPENING AND YOU'VE BEEN AGES**
- [ ] **THE DANGLER – NOTHING DROPS UNTIL YOU GIVE IT A SHAKE OR TWO**
- [ ] **BLOOD RED POOP – UNTIL YOU REMEMBER EATING BEETS**

- [ ] CLEAN POOP – NO PAPER REQUIRED
- [ ] THE FOLLOW THROUGH – YOU THOUGHT IT WAS JUST A FART
- [ ] SECOND WAVE – YOU STOOD UP ONLY TO REALISE THERE'S MORE
- [ ] SWEETCORN POOP – YUP, YOU CAN STILL SEE IT
- [ ] BOMB BLAST – PEOPLE ARE KNOCKING, ASKING IF YOU'RE OK
- [ ] AWKWARD POOP – IT'S NOT THE RIGHT TIME OR PLACE
- [ ] THE FLOATER – IT WON'T DISAPPEAR
- [ ] THE NERVOUS POOP BEFORE AN EXAM OR FIRST DATE
- [ ] THE CURRY CHASER – THE MORNING AFTER CLEAR OUT
- [ ] BUNNY BLASTER – MULTIPLE LITTLE HARD TURDS

Write down as many words as you can.
Each word must use the central letter and
be at least 3 letters long.

Write your words on the toilet paper

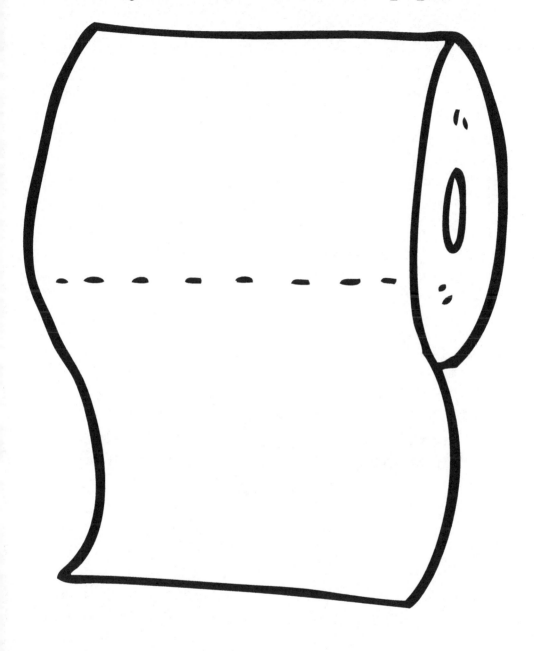

Write down 12 movie titles that describe taking a dump for example: gone with the wind

1..

2..

3..

4..

5..

6..

7..

8..

9..

10.................................

11.................................

12.................................

the
Best
Seat

in the
House

HERE I SIT

BROKEN HEARTED

TRIED TO POOP

BUT ONLY FARTED

FARTING

```
G  Z  F  D  E  A  T  H  B  R  E  A  T  H  M
L  E  T  O  N  E  R  I  P  F  K  Y  E  A  W
B  M  O  B  A  P  O  R  D  V  L  P  T  N  V
T  U  W  N  S  T  N  A  P  Y  V  A  R  G  O
U  D  E  B  A  C  K  F  I  R  E  W  M  A  J
R  S  T  I  U  C  S  I  B  S  S  A  S  E  P
D  L  O  A  O  F  L  A  T  U  L  A  T  E  R
II L  N  B  F  V  H  O  E  R  E  G  N  I  Z
O  U  E  Q  L  S  H  L  V  T  E  M  E  C  I
N  O  D  O  R  A  M  A  W  L  A  T  J  C  L
K  E  T  U  L  A  S  N  A  M  A  L  S  E  Y
P  R  U  B  M  O  T  T  O  B  K  N  F  U  J
S  S  A  P  I  R  E  W  O  L  B  N  A  E  B
S  A  G  N  O  O  M  N  A  F  P  O  O  V  D
A  Z  L  I  N  G  E  R  E  R  R  F  F  P  H  J
```

ANAL VOLCANO	DEFLATE	MAN SALUTE
ASS BISCUIT	DROP A BOMB	MOON GAS
BACKFIRE	FLAMER	ODORAMA
BEAN BLOWER	FLATULATE	PARP
BLAST OFF	GRAVY PANTS	RIP ASS
BOTTOM BURP	HONK	TURD HONK
BUSTER	LET ONE RIP	WET ONE
DEATH BREATH	LINGERER	ZINGER

A CLEAN BOWL IS OUR GOAL

SOLVE THESE ANAGRAMS

All are words for a fixed receptacle into which a person may urinate or defecate, typically consisting of a large bowl connected to a system for flushing away the waste into a sewer.

///∘\\\∘///∘\\\∘///∘\\\∘///∘\\\∘///∘\\\∘///∘\\\∘///∘\\\∘

1) ROYAL VAT ....

2) CLEAREST TWO ....

3) NICE CON EVEN ....

4) WARM SHOO.........................

5) BEND HURT OX....................

6) RODE PROM OW....................

7) SORER TOM..........................

8) SEALED HIT..........................

///∘\\\∘///∘\\\∘///∘\\\∘///∘\\\∘///∘\\\∘///∘\\\∘///∘\\\∘

Did you hear about ninja farts?

SILENT BUT DEADLY

///∘\\\∘///∘\\\∘///∘\\\∘///∘\\\∘///∘\\\∘///∘\\\∘///∘\\\∘

Answers: 1) Lavatory 2) Water Closet
3) Convenience 4) Washroom 5) Thunderbox
6) Powder Room 7) Restroom 8) The Ladies

	4				6			
8		5	1				4	
				8		1		
5		7	9	2		4		6
		3	4			2		1
4	1							5
3			8				6	4
2					9	3		
	9	8			5	7		

- -

The job isn't finished until the paperwork is done.

```
H  J  E  V  B  F  A  E  H  R  R  A  I  D  U
T  D  O  X  M  F  E  S  T  E  R  K  W  Z  N
S  W  I  D  A  A  E  T  U  F  S  D  N  Y  N
M  I  I  S  I  W  S  C  I  G  B  K  O  F  S
E  Z  B  T  G  O  R  T  U  D  N  F  C  J  T
L  T  B  J  X  U  U  A  I  L  L  U  L  P  A
L  O  Y  Y  P  U  S  S  E  C  E  F  F  S  I
Y  D  B  K  S  H  I  T  U  Z  A  N  B  S  N
F  J  D  A  N  N  U  W  I  C  A  T  T  E  I
A  X  O  M  C  I  D  I  D  N  U  V  E  E  N
R  D  E  C  G  S  T  G  C  V  G  M  G  P  G
T  J  A  M  G  E  M  S  M  Z  O  P  T  A  G
S  W  G  N  I  T  L  O  V  E  R  M  J  G  B
R  B  U  R  P  S  G  H  X  C  V  X  I  E  T
T  O  N  S  F  Z  H  D  P  E  I  X  L  T  Z
```

BURPS	FUNGUS	SCAB
DIARRHEA	MASTICATE	SEEPAGE
DISGUSTING	MUCUS	SHIT
EAR WAX	MUCUS	SMEGMA
FECES	ODIOUS	SMELLY FARTS
FECULENT	PHLEGM	SNOT
FESTER	PUS	STAINING
FETID	REVOLTING	STINKY

Fun Fact

Did you know that when you say the word "poop", your mouth makes the same motion as your asshole?.

The same is true for the phrase, "unexpected explosive diarrhoea"

Food That Passes Through

CAN YOU IDENTIFY THE FOODS IN THESE COMMON SAYINGS

----- of my eye

--- in the oven

Bring home the -----

------ someone up

Couch ------

A smart ------

Like chalk and ------

He's gone -------

Spill the -----

Selling like hot -----

Don't cry over spilled ----

Two ---- in a pod

Bigger ---- to fry

Answers: apple, bun, bacon, butter, potato, cookie, cheese, bananas, beans, cakes, milk, peas, fish

YOU NEVER KNOW WHAT YOU HAVE UNTIL IT'S GONE · LIKE · TOILET PAPER

Bathroom Riddle

I get smaller every time I have a bath.
What could I be?

Bathroom Riddle Answer - soap

Fun Things To Do In The Bathroom

1) Get sponsored to bathe in tomato soup (cold, of course) to raise money for charity

2) Wallow in a bubble bath and pretend you are in a movie

3) Learn to swim in the bath (you might need a big bath)

4) Learn something - write the things you need to learn and tape the paper to the tiles. Check it out each time you use the bathroom

5) Soap your hair up with LOTS of shampoo and make crazy new hairstyles

6) Make some scary handprints on the tiles using fake blood. Perfect for Halloween but needs more explaining at other times of the year...

7) Bob for apples at Halloween

8) Make a toy boat from trash then float it in the bath

9) Practice your snorkeling

10) Fill up your water balloons and plan your attack

SPRINKLES are for CUPCAKES not for TOILET SEATS

<u>Bathroom Riddle</u>

If there are three toilet rolls in a bathroom and you take one away, how many toilet rolls do you have?

Bathroom Riddle Answer - one - the one you took away

HASHI PUZZLE

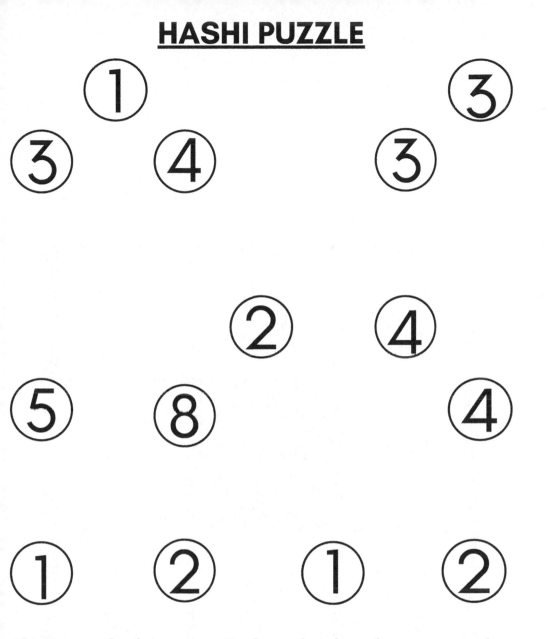

This is a single player game. Each puzzle is based on a rectangular arrangement of islands where the number in each island denotes how many bridges are connected to it. The object is to connect all islands according to the number of bridges while obeying these rules: • No more than two bridges can connect any two islands. • Bridges can only be vertical or horizontal (not diagonal) • Bridges cannot cross islands or other bridges. • When completed, all bridges should be interconnected enabling passage from island to island.

Write down as many words as you can.
Each word must use the central letter and
be at least 3 letters long.

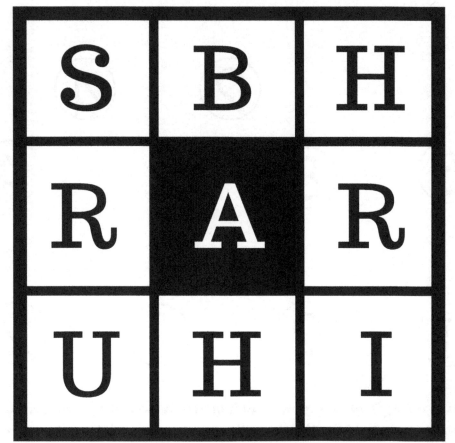

Write your words on the toilet paper

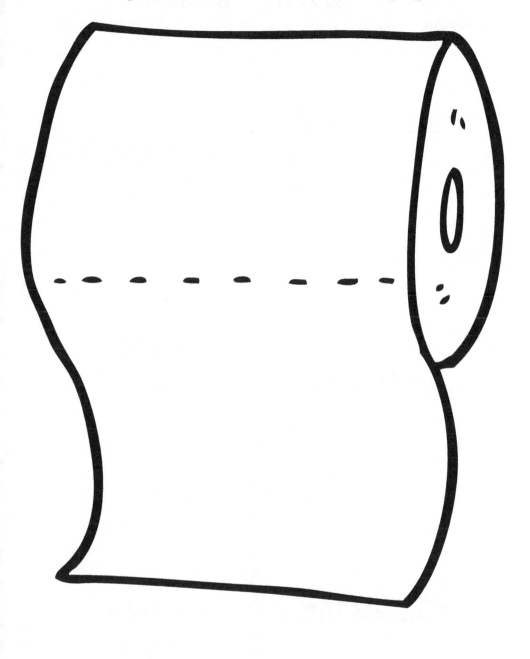

WACKY WORDS

umop apisdn

$(frozen\ water)^3$

ba n a na

MONEY
birth

OCEDROPAN

once
08:45

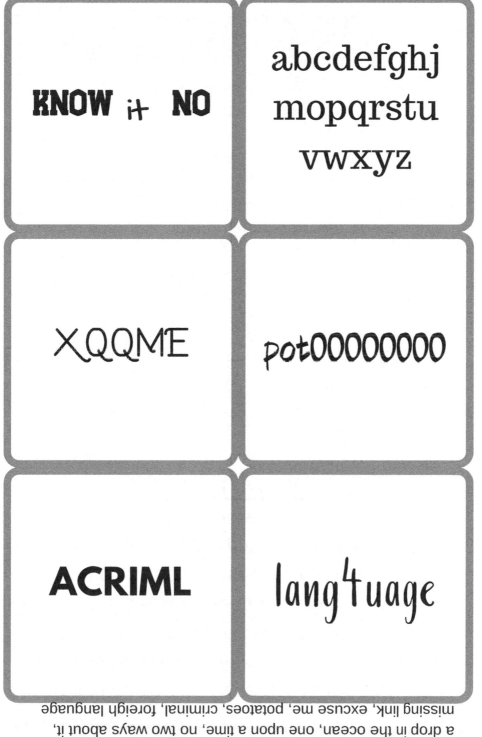

KNOW it NO

abcdefghj
mopqrstu
vwxyz

XQQME

pot00000000

ACRIML

lang4uage

Answers: upside down, ice cube, banana split, cash on delivery, a drop in the ocean, one upon a time, no two ways about it, missing link, excuse me, potatoes, criminal, foreign language

IF AT FIRST YOU DON'T SUCCEED FLUSH AGAIN

Bathroom Riddle

You are in a bathroom which has no windows. The only way to get in and out is by the door. You decide to have a bath. You close the bathroom door and lock it but the door handle breaks. The bath is quite full by now so you turn off the tap but the tap breaks and the water keeps on coming. How do you stop yourself from drowning in a room full of water?

Bathroom Riddle Answer - pull the plug

Q: What's the definition of bravery?
A: Someone with diarrhea risking a fart!

Q: Why do farts smell?
A: For the benefit of people
who are hearing impaired!

While at a party, a man farts.
Second man says "How dare you fart in
front of my wife".
First man says "Sorry, I didn't realize it
was her turn"

Q: What did the maxi pad say to the fart?
A: You are the wind beneath my wings.

Q: What do you call a dinosaurs fart?
A: A Blast from the past.

Things to say when someone asks why you have been so long in the bathroom.

```
T  V  L  O  J  G  I  H  J  U  F  F  E  F  R
H  I  N  I  I  E  L  T  K  F  X  E  L  R  Q
O  T  L  O  G  S  O  G  D  J  G  J  G  M  J
S  J  A  O  I  H  S  V  N  J  Q  N  V  L  A
T  I  X  T  R  S  T  E  P  I  K  B  U  A  V
A  L  S  N  O  G  O  N  I  T  K  L  D  T  V
G  J  V  I  K  H  K  L  I  B  P  O  J  T  S
E  Q  Y  G  R  J  S  C  P  N  M  W  H  A  T
B  P  I  H  L  C  E  A  A  X  G  O  I  C  R
E  D  I  T  P  I  R  U  L  T  E  U  Z  K  O
S  T  A  M  P  E  D  E  B  A  T  T  L  E  U
R  Q  U  A  G  M  I  R  E  L  E  A  U  D  B
B  V  Z  R  K  I  H  Z  X  Y  D  D  G  E  L
L  W  A  E  R  I  F  N  O  G  S  R  R  O  E
L  F  G  B  D  N  A  S  K  C  I  U  Q  O  D
```

ATTACKED	LIGHTNING	SHOT AT
BATTLE	LOST	STAMPEDE
BLOWOUT	NIGHTMARE	STUNG
CHOKING	ON FIRE	TROUBLE
CRISIS	ORDEAL	ZOMBIES
DOG ATTACK	QUAGMIRE	
EXPLOSION	QUICKSAND	
HOSTAGE	RIPTIDE	

Bathroom Facts - True or False?

1) Small children can drown in the toilet   True False

2) Toilets can explode   True False

3) Sewer rats can crawl up the pipes and attack an unsuspecting toilet user   True False

4) Your toilet can give you a head injury   True False

5) Straining to pass a hard poo can kill you   True False

6) In New York, so many people used the toilet at the same time that the sewer system crashed   True False

7) There is a solid gold useable toilet   True False

8) Spiders hide under airplane toilet seats then come out to bite you   True False

9) Most people have the toilet paper flap at the back touching the wall   True False

10) A toilet can sink a ship   True False

Answers on the next page

Bathroom Facts - True or False?

1) True - if they fall in head first

2) True - If you spray a toilet with something flammable   like air freshener then drop in a lighted match

3) False - this is an urban myth

4) True - perfectly possible if you slip on a wet bathroom floor and hit your head on the toilet

5) True - but thankfully very rare

6) True - it was 1983 and a very popular TV program ended (M*A*S*H, in case you were wondering) and about a million people all used the loo at the same time. Good job we can watch TV shows when we want now and not at the time they are broadcast isn't it?

7) True - the solid gold toilet was in Blenheim Palace in the UK but was sadly stolen and this caused flooding as the loo was fully operational. Worth about $6m in case you are wondering.

8) False - the cleaning chemicals would kill them although the redback spider does hide under toilet seats in Australia. It's highly venomous by the way.

9) False - 75% of people have the flap at the front - away from the wall

10) True - the toilet is a very common cause of a sinking ship as the pipes link to the outside to bring in water and flush waste. If the valves fail, too much water gets in and sinks the ship

		3		5	1		4	7
5	7	8	9			3		
			6		7			
8					2	6		
	4		1		8			
3	6	2						1
	2	9				7	6	
	3	6						8
			4	1				2

★★★

A fart is a cry for help
from an imprisoned poo

★★★

These foods might send you running to the bathroom...

```
I  E  O  C  C  S  T  I  N  K  B  U  G  S  Z
M  S  M  O  D  R  I  E  D  L  I  Z  A  R  D
K  C  O  C  J  P  S  L  R  A  K  A  H  N  Y
O  A  P  K  A  F  U  B  A  F  F  E  A  J  A
G  R  A  L  U  S  R  O  U  O  W  U  G  U  K
O  G  N  E  E  T  U  I  S  R  L  W  G  O  P
A  O  E  S  L  E  K  M  E  G  G  A  I  U  E
N  T  S  Y  T  O  D  U  A  D  G  A  S  C  N
N  I  C  A  R  S  M  E  M  R  B  E  R  M  I
A  O  Q  N  L  A  U  A  I  A  Z  R  T  I  S
T  A  P  T  X  T  U  C  C  L  A  U  A  N  A
L  C  M  Y  U  W  C  T  O  S  L  L  Z  I  A
Q  C  H  R  S  L  F  O  N  L  E  E  H  S  N
I  J  K  A  N  N  A  S  D  E  I  S  J  X  Y
O  O  L  N  T  N  T  B  E  I  C  G  H  P  E
```

AIRAG	ESCARGOT	LOCUSTS
ANT EGG SOUP	FRIED BRAIN	MOPANE
BALUT	FUGU	MUKTUK
CASU MARZU	GOANNA	SALO
CENTUARY EGG	GRUBS	SALT COD
COCKLES	HAGGIS	SANNAKJI
DRIED LIZARD	HAKARL	STINK BUGS
ESCAMOLE	JELLIED EEL	YAK PENIS

More Fun Things To Do In The Bathroom

1) Test your umbrella in the shower

2) Save the planet - stand in a large bucket as you shower then use the collected water for garden plants

3) Sing loudly and pretend you are famous

4) Experiment with wash our hair color or lots of gel

5) Write a note for your family on the bathroom mirror using washable pens

6) Pile the empty bath with pillows and create an extra bed. (Tricky when someone else wants to use the bathroom though...)

7) Make an under water movie

8) Get someone to teach you how to shave or teach someone else to shave

9) Pretend you are a pirate and shout out pirate phrases eg. 'Shiver me timbers', 'Abandon ship', 'Ooo Arrrrr' (This will cause great confusion to passers by)

10) Run a bubble bath for someone else as a nice surprise

HERE I SIT IN SMELLY VAPOUR
SOMEONE USED ALL THE PAPER
LATE FOR LUNCH BUT STILL I LINGER
BEWARE THE SMELL OF MY FINGER

LIFE IS SHORT,
EAT BURITOS

QUESTION EVERYTHING

Why?

DONT DRINK WATCR -
FISH POO IN IT

Spot the two identical bathroom bottles

no Selfies IN THE Bathroom

Bathroom Riddle

What item is round like a toilet pan, smaller than a bathtub yet a running tap will never fill it?

Bathroom Riddle Answer - a sieve

Solve these clues.
All answers contain Loo

1) Way out of a contract (6) ....

2) Produce flowers (5) ....

3) Decoration for a kids party (7) ....

4) Type O or A (5) ....

5) Partly dark (6) ....

6) Emotionally distant (5)....................

7) If you leave the tap on (5)..........................

8) Bottom of the ocean (8) ....

9) Curved piece of string (4) ....

10) House made of snow (5) ....

Answers: 1) Loophole 2) Bloom 3) Balloon 4) Blood 5) Gloomy 6) Aloof 7) Flood 8) Seafloor 9) Loop 10) Igloo

Write down as many words as you can.
Each word must use the central letter and
be at least 3 letters long.

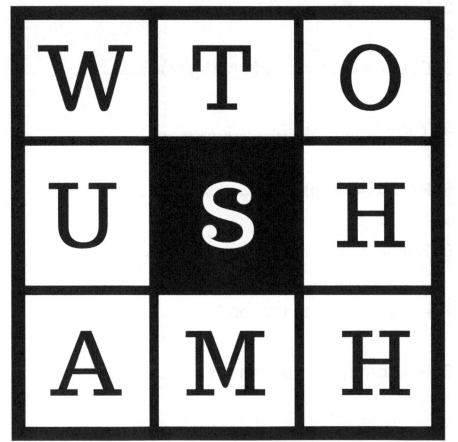

Write your words on the toilet paper

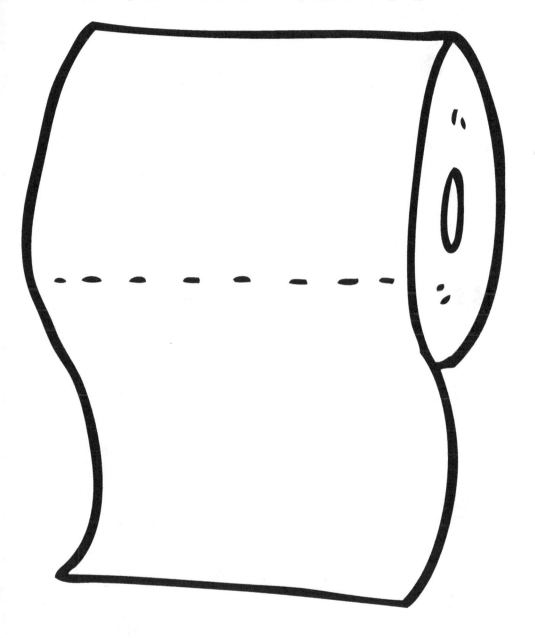

Toilet Paper Origami

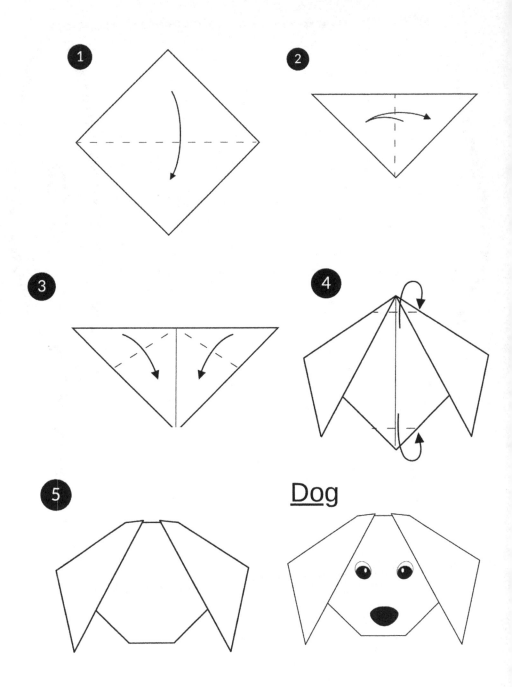

HASHI PUZZLE

This is a single player game. Each puzzle is based on a rectangular arrangement of islands where the number in each island denotes how many bridges are connected to it. The object is to connect all islands according to the number of bridges while obeying these rules: • No more than two bridges can connect any two islands. • Bridges can only be vertical or horizontal (not diagonal) • Bridges cannot cross islands or other bridges. • When completed, all bridges should be interconnected enabling passage from island to island.

Finish The Doodle

	5	9			7	1		
2		8	5		3			4
6					1		5	
	3			1		5		7
9				2		8		
						9		1
	6	4	3	9	8		1	
1					2			
					4		3	8

If I was a bubble in your bath, I'd tickle your bum and make you laugh..

Shower Spells

Get someone out of your head

Lather up your hair with shampoo and as you rub with your fingers, think of the person and recite:
'From my mind, I banish thee, Go away! Get lost! I am free'

Watch the soap suds wash away down the drain along with that person you have banished

Get rid of negative thoughts

Lather up your hair with shampoo and as you rub with your fingers recite:
'I rid myself of negative thoughts and ideas that bring me pain, I fill myself with positivity and love and happiness once again'

Sooth anxiety

Using a scented shower soap and as you wash recite:

'Flowing waters, crystal clear
Release my thoughts from all fear
Wash anxiety down the drain
Then calm and peaceful, I'll remain
Clean my body, clense my mind
Leave my worries far behind
This is my wish and my power
To feel better after this shower'

Finger Labyrinth

Use your finger to slowly trace a path to the center of the labyrinth

Breathe calmly and slowly as you focus.
When you reach the center, draw a long deep breath or two.

Then trace your path back to the outside
Repeat until you feel more focused and calm.

Focus Words

Breathe - Peace - Relax - Tranquility - Serenity - Calm - Space - Beauty
Love - Wonder - Kindness - Light - Happiness - Joy - Warmth

Observations

Are you done?

Make sure you wash your hands after reading this book....